Maria Rodale's

Organic

Gardening

Companion

Maria Rodale's

Organic

Gardening

Companion

A Seasonal Guide to Creating Your Best Garden

RODALE

We're always happy to hear from you. For questions or comments concerning the editorial content of this book, please write to:

Rodale Book Readers' Service
33 East Minor Street
Emmaus, PA 18098

Look for other Rodale books wherever books are sold. Or call us at (800) 848-4735.

For more information about Rodale and the books and magazines we publish, visit our World Wide Web site at:

www.rodale.com

Editor: Nancy N. Bailey
Cover and Interior Designer: Patricia Field
Interior Photographers: Susan Pollock (page 7) and Maria Rodale
Front Cover Photographers: Mitch Mandel (flowers and trowel) and Kurt Wilson (pencil), Rodale Images
Back Cover Photographer: Maria Rodale
Photography Editors: James A. Gallucci and Lyn Horst
Copy Editor: Jennifer Hornsby
Manufacturing Coordinator: Mark Krahforst

Rodale Organic Gardening Books
Executive Editor: Ellen Phillips
Managing Editor: Fern Marshall Bradley
Executive Creative Director: Christin Gangi
Art Director: Patricia Field
Production Manager: Robert V. Anderson Jr.
Studio Manager: Leslie M. Keefe
Associate Copy Manager: Jennifer Hornsby
Book Manufacturing Manager: Mark Krahforst

Library of Congress Cataloging-in-Publication Data
Rodale, Maria.
    [Organic gardening companion]
    Maria Rodale's organic gardening companion : a seasonal guide to creating your best garden / Maria Rodale.
        p.   cm.
    Includes bibliographical references (p.   ) and index.
    ISBN 0-87596-835-X (pbk. : acid-free paper)
    1. Organic gardening. 2. Landscape gardening. 3. Gardens—Design. 4. Seasons. I. Title.
SB453.5 .R6 1999
635'.0484—dc21   99-050469

Distributed in the book trade by St. Martin's Press

2 4 6 8 10 9 7 5 3 1   paperback

Contents

Winter

Spring

Summer

Fall

Create Your Own Dream Garden

Creating a garden is fun, exciting, challenging, soul satisfying, and, at times, frustrating. All in all, it's a very personal experience. Sure, there are a few basics that apply to any garden: following some simple rules of "good design," planting at the proper time of year, and matching plants to the right site. And as you go beyond basics, there are plenty of magazines and books to spark your creativity (including my own *Maria Rodale's Organic Gardening*). But, ultimately, the sign of a successful garden is that *you* (and your family, too) like it and feel good about where you live.

Finding happiness in your garden can only come when you've created something special that meets your unique requirements. A lot of people ask me, "How do I begin? Where do I start?" My answer is: Start right here. This book is perfect for gardeners who are just starting out.

If you're an experienced gardener, you'll enjoy using this book to keep records or to document your garden—whether you've been at it for 2 years or for 50 years. This book is meant to be written in, taped and glued into, and carried around indoors or out. Whether you want to refer back to it years later or use it to pass on your favorite ideas and garden wisdom to future generations, this is your personal companion to making your dream garden come true.

Happy organic gardening!

Maria Rodale

winter

Winter is the perfect time to create your garden plan. On a sunny winter morning, take a stroll through your yard and observe your garden in its naked glory. With flowers and foliage at a minimum, you can take a hard look at what you have, and decide what you like and what you want to change. And if your garden looks great during the winter, congratulations! It's likely to look great all year long.

A great garden starts with a carefully considered plan. If you take time to think things through now, you'll be less likely to make mistakes (which we *all* do), such as planting a tree that makes a big mess right over your patio, or making a pathway that no one seems to want to walk on because it's too far out of the way.

Planning may seem hard at first, but I've broken it down into easy steps that make it fun. And when you're done, you'll have a written record of your thoughts and preferences that you can refer back to again and again.

So find someplace comfortable, answer the questions in this chapter, and before you know it, your plan will start to take form!

How to Dream a Garden

The best gardens begin, continue, and thrive with dreaming. Even before you start picking out your favorite plants or seeds, take the time to design and plan for the coming year. Here's how to begin.

1. Spend some quiet time sitting and looking out your windows. Make yourself comfortable, have some tea, and get a blanket if you're chilly.

- What do you see?
- Are you happy with what you see?
- What do you wish you could glimpse out that window?

2. Start visualizing what you'd like to see. Think big. Don't limit your thinking to the way things are now or the way they have always been. Imagine your ideal garden. The glorious thing about your garden is that your wishes can come true.

3. **Remember all the best outdoor places you've ever loved.**

The woods, the desert, a secret walled garden, the beach, a tropical paradise, a lush British cottage garden, a farm . . . what made you love them? Of all the things you have seen and places you've been, what do you wish you could have outside your door?

4. **Now think of all the places in the world you'd love to visit.**

What seems to draw you there? Is it:

◆ water

◆ mountains

◆ your ancestral home

◆ the food

◆ the light

5. **Make a list of _every-thing_ that you'd like to have in the yard of your dreams.**

Include pictures from magazines, from your travels, and from catalogs, or even make drawings. Tape or glue them here and on the next page.

Tape pictures from catalogs and magazines here

Planting the Seeds of Your Dream Garden

The next steps get more practical but are still fun and should not be limited to reality.

1. Make a wish list of favorite flowers, vegetables, fruits, trees, shrubs, wildlife, and birds. Don't hold back. Include everything you love! Also consider your favorite color schemes.

BLEEDING HEART

Perennial Flowers

Annual Flowers

Vegetables & Herbs

Fruits & Vines

Trees & Shrubs

LEAF LETTUCE

Wildlife & Birds

2. Make a list of all the things you want to do in your yard. Here are a few suggestions to start you off:

♦ entertain

♦ relax

♦ barbecue

♦ play bocci or croquet

♦ play fetch with the dog

Add your own ideas and desires here.

3. You can also make a list of things you don't want in your yard. The things you may not want are features that take a lot of work or maintenance, invasive plants that need to be constantly cut back, or certain types of wildlife.

4. Make a list of impor-
   tant attributes.
Examples are privacy,
simplicity, formality, or
wildness—basically any-
thing that is important
to you in your yard that
hasn't shown up on any
other lists.

5. Last, make a list of
   things you feel you
   need in your yard.
You may need a certain
amount of space desig-
nated for vegetable gardening, a children's play area, a
compost area, a trash area,
a place for a shed or green-
house, or a clothesline.

What's Your Style?

Design your yard to suit your style, not mine. This book can help you to identify and create your own personal style. You'll be much happier living in an environment that reflects your own desires rather than someone else's.

Find your own style. Play! Have fun! Have no fear!

8 Steps to Make Your Dreams Come to Life

In order to follow these steps, create a sketch of your property on the graph paper on pages 20 and 21, including the buildings and yard features that exist. On layers of tissue paper overlaid on the sketch, draw the different elements that are described below.

LILY

Step 1: Start Where You Are

Take your plan, and draw in the natural environmental conditions that you have to deal with. Mark out the following general features: sunny and shady areas, directionals—north, south, east, west—winter wind directions, sloping areas, and areas that are wet or dry.

Step 2: Know Where You Have Been

Try to learn as much as you can about the history of your land and region. What zone are you in? What are the geological attributes of your region? What are your unique environmental challenges (poor soil, desert conditions, rocky soil, or sandy soil)? Now is a good time to get your soil tested. Don't forget to check for hazardous metals, especially if you live in a place where people have lived for a long time before you.

Step 3: Know Where You Are Going

Next, draw flow lines through your yard. Flow lines are the natural paths that people make from the car to the door, from the door to the shed, from the deck to the bird feeder, and so on. How do people move through your yard? To a certain extent, you can control how people move through your yard, but if you make them go too far out of their way, people will tend to make their own paths.

Step 4: Put Everything in Its Proper Place

Divide your yard into zones of usage. Put the things that are the most used and needed closest to your house and the things needed least the farthest away. For example, your kitchen and herb gardens should be as close to your kitchen as possible so that while you're cooking you can gather herbs. Site your compost pile farther away from the house in case of unsightly views or the occasional unpleasant smell (although a healthy pile doesn't smell bad at all).

Step 5: X Marks the Spot

Identify the natural areas that seem to be self-contained or already marked off in some way. Perhaps you have a hillside, a rocky area, or a wooded site. Every yard has its natural spaces. You can create spaces, too, but sometimes there are spots already there that have some magic—or some problems. The challenge and beauty is to take your dreams and work them into what you already have to make it even better.

Step 6: Take an Expedition

Find out what your native trees, wildlife, and birds are so you can incorporate them into your landscape. It helps to know what sorts of plants do well without much care. Native plants tend to feed and shelter native birds and animals. Many plants native to your area are medicinal or useful as well. A walk in the woods or a stroll by some natural hedgerows (usually growing between fields) can provide you with insight into your native plants and landscape. Take a notebook, a camera, guidebooks, sandwiches, and water, and write down what you see—and what you like.

Step 7: Commit to Your Dreams

Start applying your dreams, wishes, and favorite plants to their places, taking into consideration the specific areas you have outlined. Try not to think too much about specific plants yet. You want to be thinking about the "bones," or the underlying structure, of your yard. (Remember, bones are things like walls and large trees—the skeleton that holds the body of your yard together.) Lots of good plants can hide bad bones, but if you have good bones to begin with, almost anything will look good.

Step 8: Pick Your Plants

Now take your list of favorite plants from pages 14 and 15 and start putting them where they make sense. You will probably need a good plant field guide specifically for your region to help you. Put the shady plants you like in the shady places, and put the sun-loving plants in the gardens you have created in the sun. Can't fit the regular variety? See if it has a dwarf variety. The most important thing you can do to be a successful gardener is to put the right plant in the right place to begin with.

Record What You See in Nature's Landscape

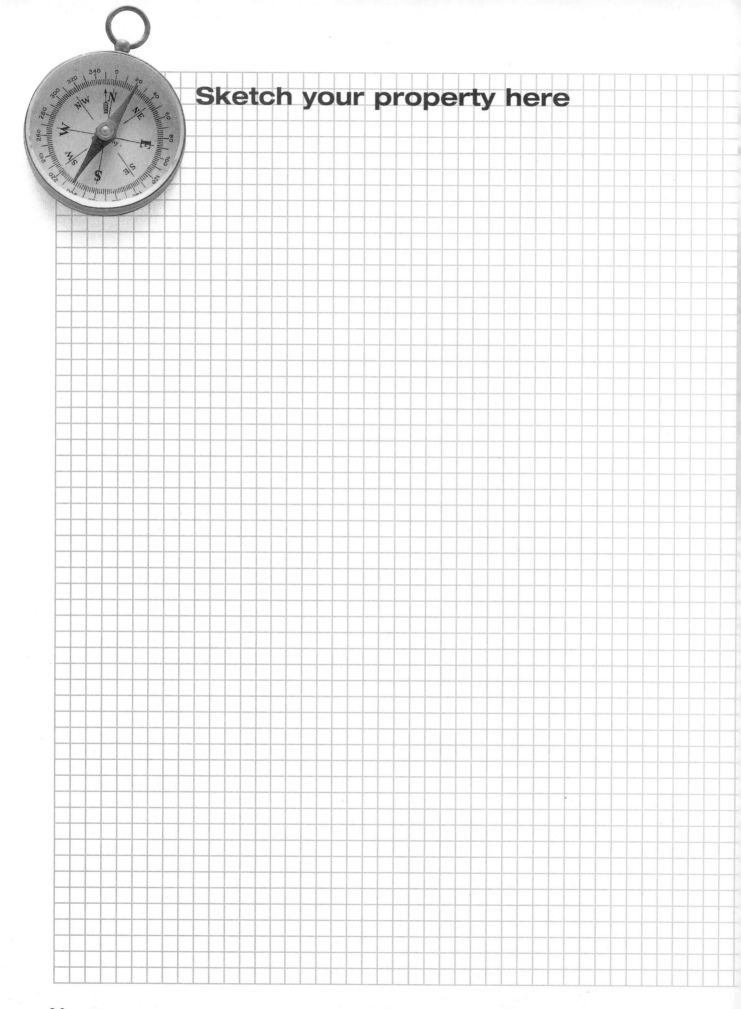

Sketch your property here

Yard Characteristics Checklist

❏ Show wet/dry areas

❏ Show sunny/shady areas

❏ Show winter wind direction

❏ Show slopes

❏ Show natural pathways through yard (flow lines)

❏ Show zones of usage

❏ Show natural areas

My Garden Stats

USDA Plant Hardiness Zone (see page 96):

_____

First frost-free date:

_____

Last frost-free date:

_____

Soil type:

_____

Soil conditions:

_____

_____

_____

Observing the Season

Take a look around. What do you like about the winter landscape—not just in your own yard, but in the environment around you? Take photos and tape them here; make sketches; write down what you see and your ideas of how it could be adapted to your space. Record what is working in your own yard, too!

Designing Especially for Winter

Here's a checklist for improving the overall design of your yard, especially in winter.

Check for eyesores.

Are there eyesores that could be concealed by a well-placed shrub, rock, or tree?

Check for privacy.

Are there open areas that need shielding?

Check for texture.

Do you have a harmonious mix of textures?

Check for color.

Find surprising ways to fit color into your winter garden.

Check for interest.

Can you break up a bleak view with a statue or tree?

Check for resting spots.

Even in winter, there should be a place to sit and reflect.

Tape photos or sketch ideas here

Ordering Seeds

The winter season is the time to plan your garden, start seedlings, and rest up for the much-anticipated warmer seasons of activity. But no ritual is more symbolic or more welcome in the dark days of winter than ordering from seed and plant catalogs.

Go to your list of favorite plants on pages 14 and 15 (and if you didn't make your list before, go back and make it now), and pick out what you want to grow this year. I like to roughly plot out my vegetable garden, for example, as I order the seeds so that I'm relatively sure I can fit everything in. You can do this on pages 26 and 27. So, settle in, go through those catalogs, and make some choices.

Tips for Success

- Be careful not to overorder plants that you haven't tried before.
- Be careful not to buy more seeds than you have time or space to start indoors.
- Focus on vegetables, fruits, and flowers that appeal to you intensely or taste better when they are homegrown.

Seed/Plant Ordering Worksheet

Use this handy chart to keep track of what you have ordered. This makes it easier to remember what to plant where when spring finally comes. (Copy this page if you need more space.)

(CATALOG COMPANY/PHONE NUMBER) _____

SEED/PLANT	ITEM #	PAGE #	PACKAGE SIZE	PRICE	COMMENTS

(CATALOG COMPANY/PHONE NUMBER) _____

SEED/PLANT	ITEM #	PAGE #	PACKAGE SIZE	PRICE	COMMENTS

Rough out your plans for vegetable and flower gardens here

PEPPERS

Planning Your Vegetable Garden

There are many ways you can go about growing vegetables and herbs, but there are three basic styles: extremely organized, totally disorganized, and somewhere in between. All three styles are completely acceptable because you can do whatever you want, however you want, in your own vegetable patch. There's no inherently wrong way to do anything. Of course, there are ways to do things that will make you more likely to succeed and to reap the juicy benefits of your efforts!

Tape pictures and plant descriptions of seeds and plants ordered from catalogs here

Starting Seedlings Timetable

If you grow some of your plants from seed, timing when to sow them can get tricky. Use the growing information on the back of each seed packet as well as your own garden's stats (see page 21) to fill in this chart.

Plant Name	Projected Set-Out Date	Seed-Starting Date	Germination Date	Actual Planting Date
10–12 Weeks from Sowing to Transplanting				
8–10 Weeks from Sowing to Transplanting				
6–8 Weeks from Sowing to Transplanting				
4–6 Weeks from Sowing to Transplanting				
2–4 Weeks from Sowing to Transplanting				

Enjoying the Season

Enjoying winter, more than any other season, is a state
of mind. It's easy to complain about the cold, damp, icy misery.
There are so many ways, however, that you can turn that
misery into a sweet, quiet joy. List some of your favorite
ways to savor winter.

◆ Drink hot chocolate.

◆ Wear thick, soft, old sweaters.

◆ Make a bouquet of winter greens and twigs.

◆ Feed the birds.

CROCUSES

Checklist for Winter

It's fun to keep track of your area's weather and see how it impacts your garden. Although your climate may not be the same as mine, to get started, you can use my reminders of what to do when.

Typical Weather for Winter Months

	December	January	February
High/low temperatures:			
Rainfall:			
Any unusual weather patterns?			

December

Planting	Harvesting	Pruning	Doing	Preparing
❑ Nothing to plant but the seeds of contentment and celebration!	❑ Cut pine boughs, other greens, berries, and branches, and pick up pinecones for holiday decorations.	❑ Survey your yard for more storm-damaged branches.	❑ Make sure your yard equipment (such as hoses), tools, and weather-sensitive pots and furniture are put away.	❑ Review garden records.
❑	❑	❑		❑ Prepare your New Year's resolutions (see page 94).
❑		❑	❑ Feed the birds.	❑
	❑		❑ Order garden-related gifts.	
❑	❑	❑	❑	❑

January

Planting	Harvesting	Pruning	Doing	Preparing
❑ If you live in a warm-season area, start seeds of perennials and cold-season vegetables, such as broccoli.	❑ When there's not too much snow on the ground (if any), walk around your yard and pick up twigs and dead branches for kindling.	❑ Survey your yard for more storm-damaged branches.	❑ Inventory your old seeds before you order new ones.	❑ Check your seed-starting supplies and make notes if you need potting soil, pots, flats, or plant growth lights.
❑ In warm-season areas, plant pansies and other spring annuals.	❑	❑	❑ Feed the birds. ❑ Check perennials for frost heaving; cover with more mulch if necessary.	❑ Clean flats and pots from last year.
❑	❑	❑	❑ Renew member-ships in garden organizations.	❑ Order seeds, perennials, herbs, trees, shrubs, and other plants from catalogs.

February

Planting	Harvesting	Pruning	Doing	Preparing
❑ Set up your equipment to start seeds.	❑ In warm climates, harvest peas, lettuce, and other crops.	❑ If you can find them, prune back raspberries.	❑ On the first nice day, get out and clean up winter debris. But don't be too fastidious. Dead plant matter makes excellent bird nest–building material and often shelters beneficial insect babies.	❑ Clean out your old gardening stuff! Inventory your tools, equipment, pots, and so on.
❑	❑	❑ Repot and fix up your indoor plants.		❑ Repair broken tools, sharpen blades, and replace things you can't fix.
❑	❑	❑ Prune deciduous trees while branches are bare of leaves and the structure is easy to see.	❑ Feed the birds.	❑
❑		❑	❑ Check to see if the groundhogs see their shadows.	

spring

Spring is the time for action. Time to get up off that couch, stride outside, and feel the life returning to the plants and soil (and your body!). If you start your garden right in spring, you'll have much less work in summer and fall. The physical work of digging and planting creates the framework of your dream garden, and for the rest of the year you can delight in watching it grow and flower.

But before you go out and willy-nilly dig, plant, and overdo it in a gardening frenzy, take the time to refine your plan. Use this chapter to design your gardens, make lists, keep track of all your plant purchases, and make sure that you have the right tools for a summer of easy outdoor living.

At first, it may seem overwhelming to get out there and start to make your garden dreams come true. But once you get started turning the soil, sowing seeds, and setting out transplants, you'll find your rhythm. Before you know it, you'll be well on your way to creating a garden masterpiece that you can build on every year, and enjoy for a lifetime.

Garden Design Layouts

Before you start to plant, take time to finalize your garden plans. I know it's hard to resist the urge to get your fingers in the ground, but you and your family will enjoy your entire yard more if you think about what you want to do. To steal a phrase, think twice, plant once. *Then* you can plant away!

Use the graph paper on pages 37 to 41 to make your detailed plans for vegetable, herb, and flower garden areas. Take the time now to plan pleasing layouts for beautiful gardens.

Jobs for the Pros

Taking into consideration time, skills, tools, and money, you may wish to hire a professional to do some of your landscaping tasks. Here are some jobs you may prefer to hire someone for:

- Cutting and trimming your lawn
- Moving around large volumes of soil
- Removing large areas of turf
- Planting and pruning large trees and shrubs
- Building stone walls, brick paths and patios, decks, and fences

Garden designs

Shopping List— Plants

Garden designs

Garden designs

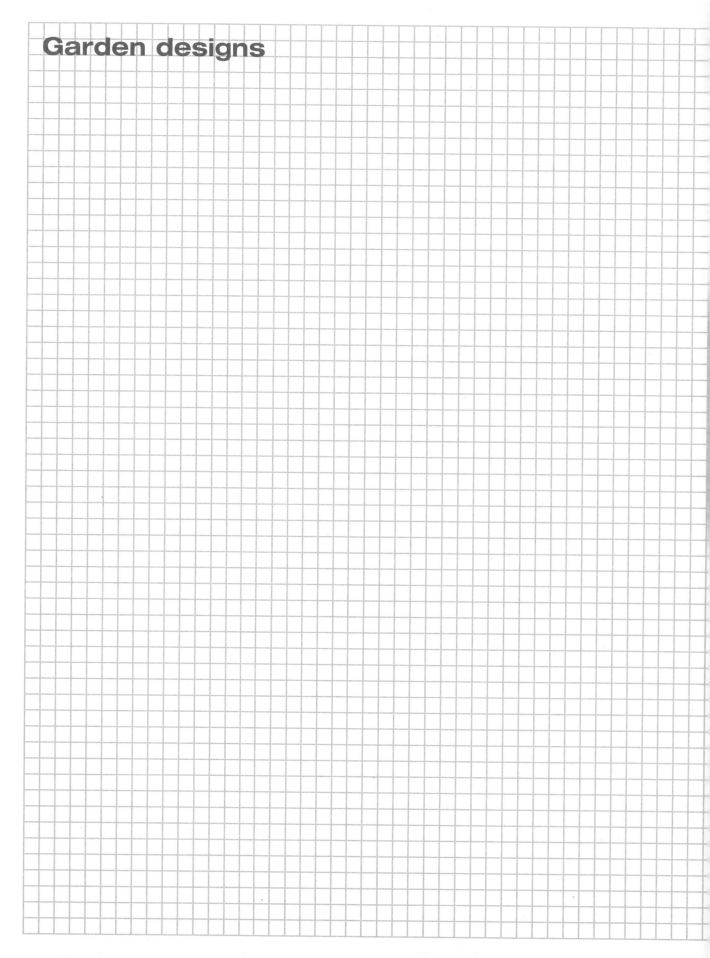

Accessories

Planting

Let the planting begin! There are other times to plant, too, but spring is the main season. It goes like this: First, plant trees and shrubs while they are still dormant (while it's still cold and before the leaves have sprouted, but after the soil has thawed). Then plant cold-season vegetables and perennial herbs and flowers. Finally, after all danger of frost has passed, plant the warm-season vegetables and annual or tender perennial herbs and flowers.

Tools Checklist

You'll need these tools to carry out most gardening tasks:

- ❏ Hedge clippers
- ❏ Hoe
- ❏ Hose and/or watering can
- ❏ Japanese weeding knife (my favorite)
- ❏ Pitchfork
- ❏ Pruners
- ❏ Rake
- ❏ Spade
- ❏ Trowel

You should also have on hand a broom for sweeping, a garden cart or wheelbarrow, garden gloves, scissors, and a weeding basket or bucket.

Planting Record—March

Planting Record—April

How to Plant

This is not difficult. Squat, dig a small hole, stick the plant in, cover with soil, and water. Putting down mulch will finish the job, adding that protective cover your plants will appreciate throughout the season. That's all there is to it. Really!

Seriously, the most important thing to consider when planting anything is to plant it in a place where it will have the conditions it likes.

BEARDED IRIS

Mulch Madness

Mulches are materials like leaves, bark, and stones that cover the ground like a blanket. Except for solid stone, they won't permanently keep other plants from growing, but they will provide a protective barrier while they decompose.

Here are the benefits of mulching.

- ◆ Mulch suppresses weeds.
- ◆ It keeps moisture in the soil.
- ◆ Mulch can increase yields.
- ◆ Plants stay cleaner and healthier.

The most popular and best mulches are compost, grass clippings, bark mulch and other wood mulches, straw, and chopped leaves. Use those that are close by, locally made, and organic or as natural as possible.

Planting Record—May

Compost—The Secret Ingredient of Great Gardens

Compost is not only essential to provide your soil with great nutrients, but it is also practical, easy, and efficient. Think of composting as your home waste disposal system that results in a product 100 percent recycled and 100 percent valuable in your garden.

Composting does not have to be complicated. You *can* compost simply—find a good place for a pile in a part of your yard that is hidden from view, and just dump sticks, weeds, kitchen waste, and garden waste there. Add cow, horse, or other farm-animal manure (from a source that you know is organic, hormone-free, and healthy), *if* you can get it. If not, no big deal.

Compost dos and don'ts

Typically, compost is made up of these three things; you can add any of these ingredients to your pile.

- carbon: dry leaves, chipped wood, sticks, straw, paper
- nitrogen: grass clippings, weeds, garden trimmings, kitchen scraps
- soil: the soil on plant roots contributes the microbes that will cause the other materials to break down

Here are the things that you shouldn't put on your pile:

- meat or animal products
- grains
- bread
- oils or fats
- anything toxic, non-biodegradable, or poisonous
- dog or cat waste
- weeds that have gone to seed or have strong root systems
- diseased plants

Observing the Season

Here's a place to observe what you like about the spring landscape—not just in your own yard, but also in the environment around you. Take photos and tape them here; plan your strategy for getting what you like into your space.

Designing Especially for Spring

Plant for early signs of life. Nothing warms the soul like bulbs popping up from the cold earth in February and March.

Plant for bloom power. Spring-blooming bushes, flowers, and trees can be tacky and glorious at the same time. Spring can be absolutely psychedelic.

Plant for heady fragrance. Nothing banishes the ghosts and darkness of winter like the sweet smell of spring (see page 51).

Plant for the eradication of winter. A garden filled with spring-blooming plants makes the past winter seem like a strange dream you can barely remember on waking.

Tape photos or sketch ideas here

Tape photos or sketch ideas here

Ideas for Improvements

When you're drinking in the sights and smells of the spring landscape, take some time to note what you like and don't like—while the plants are blooming. Then when you are ready to move or plant bulbs, perennials, or groundcovers, you'll have your strategy right in front of you. Since most bulbs are planted in the fall or best moved then, it's often hard to remember what thoughts you had back in spring. Use this chart to help keep a record of what you want to do.

TULIP

Perennial or Bulb	Where It Is Now	Where I Want to Add It/Move It

Perennial or Bulb	Where It Is Now	Where I Want to Add It/Move It

Spring's Most Fragrant Plants

These plants top my list for delicious spring fragrance. There's room for at least one or two in every garden.

- ❏ Fragrant daffodils
- ❏ Daphne
- ❏ Honeysuckles
- ❏ Hyacinths
- ❏ Lavenders
- ❏ Lemon balm
- ❏ Lemon grass
- ❏ Lilac
- ❏ Lily-of-the-valley
- ❏ Mints
- ❏ Mock oranges
- ❏ Peonies
- ❏ Rosemary
- ❏ Roses
- ❏ Star magnolias
- ❏ Sweet shrub
- ❏ Viburnums

Bird and Butterfly Journal

Checklist of Birds in Your Backyard

Keep a checklist of birds you've spotted in your yard as well as when you're out and about. Once you've figured out most of the common birds in your area, you may want to learn about others.

- ❏ Mourning dove
- ❏ Northern cardinal
- ❏ Dark-eyed junco
- ❏ American crow
- ❏ House finch
- ❏ Bluejay
- ❏ Black-capped chickadee
- ❏ Downy woodpecker
- ❏ American goldfinch
- ❏ Tufted titmouse
- ❏ Sparrow
- ❏ Nuthatch
- ❏ Hummingbird
- ❏ Robin
- ❏ Mockingbird
- ❏ European starling
- ❏ Canada goose
- ❏ Common grackle
- ❏ Red-winged blackbird
- ❏ Wren

Keep a bird and butterfly journal and count the species that come to visit (the more the merrier!). Keep a good set of identification books and binoculars handy. You may even keep an eye out for where birds build their nests.

Bird Description	Where Observed	Date

Butterfly/Caterpillar Description	Where Observed	Date

Attract Birds and Butterflies

- Plant climbing vines like trumpetvine or wisteria.
- Plant nectar-, seed-, and berry-producing plants, such as cherries, crabapples, dogwoods, hawthorns, serviceberries, many evergreens, hollies, viburnums, black-eyed Susans, and cardinal flowers, to name a few.
- Caterpillars also have food preferences. For example, black swallowtail caterpillars prefer plants like dill, Queen-Anne's-lace, and parsley.
- Put out a birdbath or shallow bowl filled with water.
- Dust keeps parasites under control, so leave a little dust patch for birds to bathe in.

Enjoying the Season

Here are some of my favorite ways to celebrate the arrival of spring.

- The daily tour: Take a tour around your yard every day (before or right after work for a special dose of strength and peace) to see "what's up." In those first days of spring, the changes are dramatic and hopeful.
- Plant trees in memory of people or pets.
- Plan an outdoor picnic or party to give yourself a deadline to get the yard ready and planted for summer.
- On a rainy spring day, put on your rubber boots and raincoat, grab an umbrella, and head to your local nursery for a walk and to peruse the new stock. Buy some plants and get all wet.
- Let your kids pick out and plant a tree or bush from the local nursery. Most kids love to dig, and it gives them something to remember for a long time.
- Make your first spring salad and savor every bite!

How do you like to celebrate spring?

Basic Spring Vinaigrette Salad with Violets

Violets add a delightful splash of color and spicy flavor to this salad.

Greens, picked fresh

3 parts good olive oil

1 part good vinegar (preferably wine vinegar)

Pinch of kosher salt

Freshly ground pepper

Violets, rinsed gently

1. Wash and dry any type of spring greens or a combination.

2. Put the oil, vinegar, salt, and pepper in a small bowl (I just use a small cereal bowl), starting with the oil. Emulsify with a fork (whip it up as if scrambling an egg). You can add any extras that you like: herbs, garlic, shallots, or whatever.

3. Pour the dressing on the greens, and toss them. Sprinkle the violets on top. Enjoy!

Checklist for Spring

It's fun to keep track of your area's weather and see how it impacts your garden. Although your climate may not be the same as mine, to get started, you can use my reminders of what to do when.

Typical Weather for Spring Months

	March	April	May
High/low temperatures:			
Rainfall:			
Any unusual weather patterns?			

March

Planting	Harvesting	Pruning	Doing	Preparing
❏ It's time to plant peas, trees, shrubs, and early perennials.	❏ Harvest dandelions for an early spring salad.	❏ Prune dead branches on trees and shrubs and dead canes on roses.	❏ Apply compost to your garden.	❏ Prepare to plant— get your seeds, seedlings, and plant lists in order.
❏	❏ In the South, harvest peas, radishes, and lettuce.	❏ Cut back any perennials that look messy.	❏ Get your garden furniture out of winter storage and clean it off.	❏
❏	❏	❏	❏ Clean up debris left from last year or from winter damage.	❏
❏	❏	❏	❏ Turn under cover crops.	❏
			❏ Finalize your catalog orders of shrubs, perennials, and other plants.	

April

Planting	Harvesting	Pruning	Doing	Preparing
❑ Set out transplants of broccoli, cauliflower, and cabbage.	❑ Harvest asparagus and rhubarb.	❑ Cut back ornamental grasses if you haven't already done so.	❑ Do your first round of weeding while the weeds are still small.	❑ Put away your snow shovel and other reminders of winter.
❑ Plant lettuce, kale, chard, radish, and carrot seeds directly in the garden.	❑	❑ Thin raspberry canes. Cut out dead canes.	❑ Dig new garden beds.	❑
❑ Plant seed potatoes.	❑	❑	❑ Edge all your garden beds, or decide once and for all to put permanent edging in.	❑
❑ Plant more new shrubs and trees.	❑	❑	❑ Mow the lawn for the first time.	❑
❑ Plant a new strawberry bed.				

May

Planting	Harvesting	Pruning	Doing	Preparing
❑ Plant vegetables.	❑ Pick peas, strawberries, more rhubarb, and lettuces.	❑ Prune spring-flowering shrubs such as forsythia and lilacs when they're done flowering.	❑ Plant in containers and window boxes.	❑ Start a new compost pile.
❑ Plant annuals. Use annuals to try out a design scheme. If you like it, plant similar perennials there next year.	❑ Make sure you eat your vegetables and fruits—they are not just growing to look beautiful!	❑ Don't cut off daffodils and tulips after blooming. Let the leaves die a natural death, and you will be rewarded with richer soil and better bloom next year. Plant groundcovers, annuals, or perennials around them.	❑ Cut lilacs, peonies, and sweet peas for indoor bouquets.	❑ Take an inventory of your canning supplies and freezer containers.
❑ Plant perennials.			❑	❑
❑ Plant herbs.	❑		❑	❑
❑	❑			

summer

Summertime is the ultimate test of a good garden. If being out in your garden makes you happy even during the hottest, buggiest, and weediest months of the year, then consider your plan a success.

A great summer garden has shade—for you and your house. It also has places to nap and relax at any time of day. It's fully planted and mulched so that it needs very little maintenance. And it's built to withstand the extremes of weather, from droughts to floods.

A great summer garden also teems with life. Birds, butterflies, ladybugs, and crickets will make your garden work for you while providing priceless entertainment.

This chapter will help you plan and create a garden that is meant for good living, observe all the wild activity, and reflect on family and having fun. And if you resist the temptation of spraying chemicals, you'll reap the benefits of an intricate balance of natural controls that no scientist could ever re-create artificially. Relax, have yourself a cool drink, and imagine life as it was meant to be. You can make it happen!

Keeping Up with Maintenance

Summer can be a bit daunting in the garden if your weeds and troubles exceed your flowers and joys. By planting thickly and mulching thoroughly, most of the worst work can be avoided. However, weeding is a fact of life if you are going to have a garden. And weed killers cause a lot more problems than they solve. Therefore, you may as well find a way to enjoy the process. Here are my tips.

- **If you remember only one thing:** Pull the weeds out by the *roots*. Just ripping them off at the stems will only lead to stronger, deeper-rooted weeds that are harder to pull.

- **Best time to weed:** early morning. By early, I mean between sunrise and 8:30 A.M.

- **Second-best time to weed:** late afternoon and early evening. Sometimes after work it's just what the doctor ordered to change into something comfortable and get out there and pull. It's the most beautiful, relaxed time of the day in the garden.

- **Worst time to weed:** anytime it's too hot, humid, buggy, or dry. Also avoid thunder, lightning, hail, and hurricanes.

- **Best time for the soil to be weeded:** After a soaking rain, weeds pull out of the dirt like ripe apples falling out of a tree.

- **Note of caution about weeding when plants are wet:** Some things should not be touched, picked, or weeded when wet. Weeding carrots when they are wet causes the scent to attract carrot flies. Touching green beans when they are wet can cause rust (a fungal disease) on the beans and leaves.

- **Best tools:** two baskets—one large one for the weeds and the other for the tools (weeding knife, scissors for deadheading, and raffia for tying things up and back). When the weed basket is full, dump it on the compost pile.

- **Best weeding system:** Start at one point and work around from there. Set a goal for yourself—from the porch to a certain tree, for example. Tell yourself, "As soon as I get to that tree, I will quit." For some reason, the closer I get to the tree, the easier the weeding goes, and I usually end up going past my goal.

- **Best weeding rule to live by:** Never let a weed go to seed. Ever hear the old saying, "One year's seed is seven years' weed"? It sure seems true.

What Are *Your* Weedy Areas?

Take a hard look at the areas that cause you the most weeding or other maintenance headaches. Where are they and what are some possible solutions?

_____

_____

_____

_____

_____

_____

_____

_____

_____

_____

_____

_____

_____

_____

_____

_____

_____

_____

_____

_____

_____

_____

_____

_____

_____

_____

_____

Natural Lawn Care

The key to a successful, non-wasteful lawn is to plant a mix of seed varieties and then not get obsessed with it. The more you baby it, the more it will act like a baby.

- **Mowing.** Don't cut the grass shorter than 3 inches. Leaving it a bit longer encourages deeper root growth, so the lawn needs less watering (if any). Use the clippings as mulch, use a mulching mower, or just leave the grass on the lawn!

- **Fertilizing.** Not necessary, but if you do it, use organic fertilizers. Better to plant the right grass for your climate.

- **Watering.** If you must, water in the morning, and do it infrequently but deeply.

- **Weeds.** Lots of weeds (including the infamous dandelion) are a symptom of a deeper problem—the wrong kind of grass, compacted soil, bad mowing practices. Find and fix the root of the problem and you'll rid your lawn of most weeds.

Structures and Accessories for Your Garden

Plants are wonderful, of course, but for a really great-looking garden—and a garden that's fun to be in—you need structures and accessories, too. Whether it's a deck or patio to relax on, a bench to sit on, a fence to mark a boundary, or an arbor for shade and beauty, you'll get more four-season pleasure from a well-accessorized garden. Use this list to decide how your structures are working for you.

Porches

Patios and decks

Gazebos

Arbors and pergolas

Fences

My Garden Structure Wish List

Garden furniture

Garden art

Garden lighting

Water features

Window boxes

Hanging baskets

Freestanding pots

Observing the Season

When thinking about summer in the garden, certain things come to mind: shady places to hang out on lazy days, peaceful places to de-stress after a hard day's work, low-maintenance gardens (you don't want to spend your whole summer weeding, mowing, and trimming, do you?), a place to picnic or have dinner outside, a place to soak in the sun, and a place that's beautiful to look at and be in—whether you're going to entertain or just enjoy it all by yourself.

DAISY

Ask yourself if your summer garden satisfies your desires.

◆ Are there shady places to sit and relax?

◆ Is there a place to have meals outside that is actually comfortable to use?

◆ Do the plants surprise and delight you?

◆ Are there good things to eat?

◆ Does taking a little walk around your yard to see what is growing give you a thrill of excitement and anticipation?

In addition to asking yourself the above questions, take the time to observe what plants are thriving . . . and which are not. What combinations are working . . . and which are not? Use photos, sketches, and words on the next few pages to evaluate what is happening in your yard in summer.

◆ Use annuals to test color or planting schemes. If you like the way they look, find similar perennials to plant next year or in the fall. For instance, if you are looking for a purple flower, try annual purple salvia. If you like the way it looks, switch to a perennial such as lavender, Russian sage, or veronica.

◆ Don't go hog-wild buying tons of one perennial if you haven't planted it before. Some perennials just don't do that well in some yards, and others do surprisingly well. If one does well, then next year go hog-wild!

◆ Don't be afraid to move things around. If you don't like how something looks after it grows, move it somewhere else.

◆ Be adventurous—try a few new plants if they look interesting. That's the fun of gardening!

◆ A money-saving tip: Go to nurseries in midsummer and buy perennials on sale. Fill in bare spots with them this year, and then watch them explode with color next year!

Getting to Know Your Bugs

Bugs play a critical role in the garden. They eat waste, break it down into fertilizer, provide food for birds and animals who also fertilize your garden, eat other bugs, and do a lot of soil aeration and improvement. By human standards, there are definitely bugs that are considered good and others that are considered bad. And it has nothing to do with looks. Trying to eradicate all bugs will only give the bad bugs an advantage by making them even more resilient.

EARTHWORMS

DRAGONFLY

ANT

BEE

SPIDER

PRAYING MANTID

Heroes of the Garden

The first step of working in partnership with bugs is to recognize the ones that are actually garden heroes. Check all the ones you are lucky enough to find in your garden.

Insect	Where Seen	Date
❑ ants		
❑ assassin bugs		
❑ bees		
❑ ground beetles		
❑ lady beetles		
❑ mealybug destroyers		
❑ soldier beetles		
❑ doodlebugs		
❑ dragonflies		
❑ earthworms		
❑ fireflies		
❑ green lacewings		
❑ minute pirate bugs		
❑ praying mantids		
❑ predatory mites		
❑ robber flies		
❑ spiders		
❑ syrphid flies		
❑ tachinid flies		
❑ wasps		

Pesty Bugs

Besides being a problem, these pests may point to a larger problem in your garden. They are fair game for all the bug-beating strategies you can bring to bear on them—nonchemically, of course!

Insect	Where Seen	Date
❑ aphids		
❑ beetles		
❑ borers		
❑ grasshoppers		
❑ leafhoppers		
❑ treehoppers		
❑ maggots and flies		
❑ mealybugs		
❑ mites		
❑ scale		
❑ slugs and snails		
❑ thrips		
❑ weevils		
❑ worms and caterpillars		

WORM

BEETLE

FLY

GRASSHOPPER

SNAIL

Happy-Go-Lucky Garden Pedestrians

These creatures are neither friend nor foe—they're just along for the ride. Enjoy them for their songs and for adding diversity to your yard—and maybe for providing a meal or two for hungry birds along the way. Check all the ones you can identify.

Insect	Where Seen	Date
❑ centipedes and millipedes		
❑ cicadas		
❑ field crickets		
❑ earwigs		
❑ katydids		
❑ moths		
❑ spittlebugs		
❑ walking sticks		

MOTH

CRICKET

CICADA

Harvesting

Keeping notes on the successes and failures of your garden plants is a valuable way to evaluate the decisions you made in winter. Learn to benefit from your successes *and* failures by recording your harvests as well as by evaluating the performance of your plants.

Flower:

Performance:

Susceptibility to insects/diseases:

Would I plant this variety again?
Why/why not?

Flower:

Performance:

Susceptibility to insects/diseases:

Would I plant this variety again?
Why/why not?

Flower:

Performance:

Susceptibility to insects/diseases:

Would I plant this variety again?
Why/why not?

Vegetable/Fruit/Herb:

Date harvesting begins/ends:

Quantity:

Comments:

Would I plant this variety again?

Why/why not?

Vegetable/Fruit/Herb:

Date harvesting begins/ends:

Quantity:

Comments:

Would I plant this variety again?

Why/why not?

Vegetable/Fruit/Herb:

Date harvesting begins/ends:

Quantity:

Comments:

Would I plant this variety again?

Why/why not?

Vegetable/Fruit/Herb:

Date harvesting begins/ends:

Quantity:

Comments:

Would I plant this variety again?

Why/why not?

Vegetable/Fruit/Herb:

Date harvesting begins/ends:

Quantity:

Comments:

Would I plant this variety again?

Why/why not?

Vegetable/Fruit/Herb:

Date harvesting begins/ends:

Quantity:

Comments:

Would I plant this variety again?

Why/why not?

Vegetable/Fruit/Herb:

Date harvesting begins/ends:

Quantity:

Comments:

Would I plant this variety again?

Why/why not?

Vegetable/Fruit/Herb:

Date harvesting begins/ends:

Quantity:

Comments:

Would I plant this variety again?

Why/why not?

Vegetable/Fruit/Herb:

Date harvesting begins/ends:

Quantity:

Comments:

Would I plant this variety again?

Why/why not?

Flower:

Performance:

Susceptibility to insects/diseases:

Would I plant this variety again?

Why/why not?

Flower:

Performance:

Susceptibility to insects/diseases:

Would I plant this variety again?

Why/why not?

Flower:

Performance:

Susceptibility to insects/diseases:

Would I plant this variety again?

Why/why not?

Flower:

Performance:

Susceptibility to insects/diseases:

Would I plant this variety again?

Why/why not?

Family Heritage Gardening

Summer is often a time of family reunions. Instead of talking about everyone's latest ailments or sports, ask about favorite family recipes, gardening tips, and plants with special meaning for your family tree.

Fill in the
leaves with
names of
your
ancestors.

Wildlife Journal

Instead of being suspicious each time you see furry creatures in your yard, observe their behavior. You'll enjoy wildlife more if you know a little about them. You can also sketch or take photos and tape them to these pages. Who knows—you might take an award-winning photo!

Animal Observed	Comments

Animal Observed	Comments

How to Keep Wildlife Out

Introduce predators. Having dogs and cats can do wonders to keep away animals.

Plant things they won't eat. If rabbits get your peas every time, then don't plant them. Plant trees and shrubs that deer don't like, such as azaleas, boxwood, butterfly bush, junipers, oleander, and rhododendrons.

Use HavaHart traps. Catch the animals and then take them to a wild place to free them. Or call your local animal control officer to take over.

Try natural sprays, sonic devices, remedies, and repellents. Reapply the sprays after every rain.

Build barriers and fences. The only foolproof way to keep out the big animals like deer and woodchucks is to fence high (up to 9 feet) and low (3 feet underground—for woodchucks, not deer).

Enjoying the Season

Summer is such an obvious time for enjoyment. What are your favorite ways to enjoy summer?

- ◆ Catch fireflies in a jar to make a fairy-tale lantern. Release them at the end of the evening.
- ◆ Play "freestyle" badminton without a net.
- ◆ Make sun tea with fresh mint or herbal tea bags.

COSMOS

NASTURTIUMS

Have a Garden Party!

Put this book down right now and have a party. Nothing fancy—cook whatever is ripe, uncork a bottle of wine, light some citronella candles in jelly jars. Talk about things. Important things. Silly things. Take off your shoes. Let the dishes go until tomorrow. Invite someone you would like to get to know better. If there isn't anybody you'd like to get to know better, have the party for yourself or your family. The crickets will be sure to come.

Checklist for Summer

It's fun to keep track of your area's weather and see how it impacts your garden. Although your climate may not be the same as mine, to get started, you can use my reminders of what to do when.

Typical Weather for Summer Months

	June	July	August
High/low temperatures:			
Rainfall:			
Any unusual weather patterns?			

June

Planting	Harvesting	Pruning	Doing	Preparing
❑ Plant succession plantings of beans, carrots, summer lettuces, and cilantro.	❑ Harvest whatever is ready—herbs, beans, peas, strawberries, greens, and beyond.	❑ Prune spring-flowering shrubs—if you need to.	❑ Keep birdbaths clean and filled with water.	❑ Prepare to move all of your eating and entertaining outdoors.
	❑	❑	❑ Weed now before August hits and things really get out of control.	❑ Cut bouquets of roses and perennials for family and guests.
❑ Fill in any bare spots with annuals, perennials, or leftover seeds.		❑	❑ Make sure everything is mulched.	❑
	❑		❑ Start a new compost pile.	
❑ Plant brussels sprout transplants for fall harvests.		❑		❑
❑	❑		❑ Set out beer traps for slugs.	

July

Planting	Harvesting	Pruning	Doing	Preparing
❑ Plant last-minute purchases of plants on sale. (Water them well for the first week or so if it doesn't rain.)	❑ Harvest herbs for drying.	❑ Deadhead flowers that have already bloomed to stimulate new blooms.	❑ Take a daily tour of your yard.	❑ Preserve fruits in jams, sauces, and desserts.
	❑ Make herb vinegars for Christmas gifts.		❑ Weed, weed, weed!	❑ Make a batch of dill pickles.
❑ Plant succession crops of cilantro and heat-tolerant lettuces.	❑ Make onion and garlic braids.	❑ Prune evergreen hedges.	❑ Find a neighbor who doesn't have any zucchini—and likes it.	❑
❑ Plant broccoli, cabbages, and cauliflower seedlings for fall harvests.	❑ Pick the first tomato!	❑ Prune wisteria to control its spread and to encourage spring blooming.	❑ Remove diseased plants. (Don't compost them.)	
	❑ Harvest beans, cucumbers, and squash before they get humongous.	❑		❑
❑ Sow kale.			❑ Handpick pests—especially Japanese beetles from roses.	

August

Planting	Harvesting	Pruning	Doing	Preparing
❑ Sow final fall succession plants: Chinese greens, lettuces, peas, radishes, spinach and turnips.	❑ Harvest beans, melons, potatoes, and tomatoes.	❑ Prune diseased or broken branches on trees and shrubs.	❑ Try not to give up.	❑ Freeze corn.
			❑ Watch out for heat stroke!	❑ Make pesto.
❑	❑ Harvest early apples, blackberries, elderberries, peaches, and peppers.	❑	❑ Take notes on plants that perform well.	❑ Roast peppers and freeze them.
				❑ Make tomato sauce to freeze.
	❑ Harvest everything! Continue to deadhead annuals and perennials.	❑	❑ Pull weeds before they go to seed.	❑ Can salsa.
❑			❑ Save the seeds from your heirloom tomatoes.	❑ Can peaches.
	❑	❑		❑
			❑ Order fall bulbs for planting.	

fall

Harvest time! For thousands of years, fall has been a celebration of bounty from the garden and from nature. Pumpkins, apples, grapes, tomatoes, herbs, and fall's final flowers are some of those wonderful rewards for all your planning and planting efforts.

This chapter will help you prepare for winter, preserve your harvest, and reflect on what you may want to do differently in your garden next year. Fall is a good time for recording your thoughts about the past year, planning what you're going to do next year, and scheming about how to make your dream garden even more real.

Doing too much to your garden in fall can actually be harmful. The last thing you should be doing is cutting back all your plants or raking everything to obsession. The luxurious mess of a densely planted garden is the overwintering ground for many of your garden allies, including birds, lady beetles, and other beneficials. To keep your garden in its proper natural balance, you need to let go and let nature work for you.

It's time to get out there and enjoy that final fall show.

Observing the Season

I don't think we gardeners are ever satisfied.
There's always something we want to try or change in our yards.
Thank goodness! And fall is a great time to review and refine your
landscape design. Ask yourself these questions every fall—it will
help your garden get better and better each year.

1. Are things planted in
   the right location?

2. What did really well?

3. What weren't you
   satisfied with?

4. Where did you end up weeding too much?

5. What else was high maintenance?

6. What didn't do well?

7. Are there bare spots you may want to fill in with bulbs, ground-covers, perennials, shrubs, or trees?

Start Your Plan for Next Year

When the snow starts to fall, you'll have a hard time remembering where you needed to plant those spring flowers or what plants you wanted to get to fill in your garden. Don't forget about vegetable rotation, too. Don't plant your potatoes in the same place as the previous year, or the bugs will eat them before you can.

So take notes now. Soak up some vitamin D. Make a list. Sketch out some ideas. Review this book for other notes you've taken (especially on pages 46 to 51), and incorporate some of those ideas here.

Think about how you want to use your yard differently, too. Think about paths and walkways. Are they in the right spot? Go with the flow.

Or perhaps you want to try some new techniques or projects in your yard. What have you observed on walks in your neighborhood, on vacations, or in the woods that has inspired you?

Garden plan

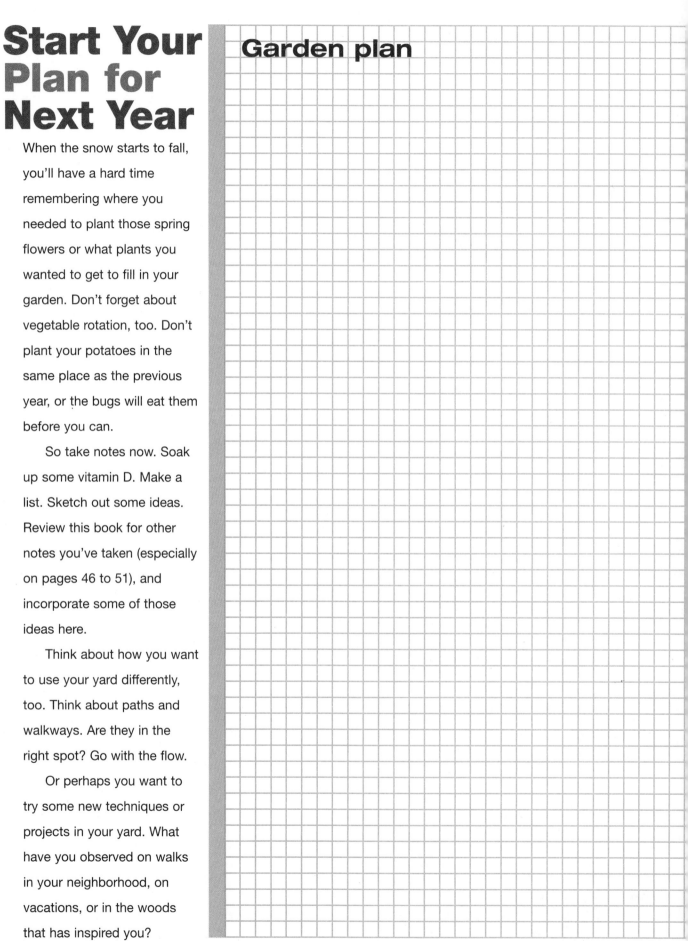

Buying and Planting in Fall

Taking a trip to a nursery in the fall to buy trees and shrubs can be frustrating. Nurseries tend to sell plants with nice fall foliage rather than a selection of plants for all seasons. And even though fall is a great time to plant all sorts of trees, nurseries will have sold out of many of them last May. However, some nurseries offer great bargains in fall.

The fall catalogs actually offer a much larger selection of plants with no difference in quality—in fact, quality is often better. You'll find lots of bulbs that should be planted in the fall as well as all those fabulous spring- and summer-flowering trees and shrubs. Fall is also when ornamental grasses are in their glory, so this is a natural time to look at what's available in the catalogs.

Bulbs

Perennials

Trees & Shrubs

Designing Especially for Fall

- ◆ Choose a few trees and shrubs that stand out just because of their fall color. Plant them where their color is highlighted by the surrounding plants, such as a background of evergreens.

- ◆ Mums are nice, but don't overdo it. There are lots of other ways to get color into your landscape. Hydrangeas and asters are especially lovely.

- ◆ Keep planting cool-season vegetables, such as arugula, corn salad, kale, radishes, spinach, and turnips, into September. Lettuce mixes do very well in September and October (until the first frost), and they also add that fresh green color to your landscape.

- ◆ Include fall fruits in your plantings. There are many apple varieties that are disease-resistant. Quinces are beautiful and delicious in the fall. 'Fallgold' raspberries are my favorites.

Preserving Your Harvest

There is no better feeling than heading into winter with food from your garden nestled in the freezer, lined up on the shelves, and dried or canned in your pantry.

Foods Frozen	Date	Yield

My Best Preserving Techniques

Foods Dried	Date	Yield

Foods Canned	Date	Yield

Other Foods Made	Date

General Preserving Tips

Here are a few tips to help you become a preserving pro. Don't forget: Homemade jams, jellies, pickles, and applesauce make great gifts.

◆ Preserve your best, most perfect foods. A bad piece of fruit will taste just as bad frozen, canned, or dried, and it can spoil the whole batch.

◆ If you want to make jams and jellies, use fruit that is not quite ripe because it has a higher pectin content.

◆ Another method of storing foods is called root cellaring. If you have one of those cellar doors with an underground covered entrance, you can use the inside as a cold-storage room during winter months. Just put your cabbages, potatoes, carrots, and other roots and fruits in mouse- and pest-proof containers. (Store your apples and pears in a separate area from the vegetables because the ethylene gas released by the fruit will cause your potatoes to sprout.)

Record Your Favorite Recipes

In my book *Maria Rodale's Organic Gardening,* I share many of my favorite seasonal recipes. Record some of your favorites of the seasons here.

My Philosophy on Food

1. Eat food that's as fresh as possible. Scientifically, this is important because nutrients in the food are more potent when the food is fresh. Spiritually, I feel as if I am gathering life strength and vitality from the aliveness of fresh food. Try it, and you'll see what I mean.

2. Eat as organically as possible. Scientifically, there may still be no conclusive proof that chemicals are not harmful to human health, but they're definitely harmful for the environment. Spiritually, you can eat organic foods knowing that you are not harming the earth, other people, or your children.

3. Eat food as unprocessed as possible. The closer it is to its original form, the more nutrients, the more life, and the more fiber will be in the food.

4. Eat all things in moderation. Balance, moderation, and variety are key.

5. Indulge yourself occasionally. If you have a strong base of healthy living, a few indulgences won't hurt you. No one is perfect—nor should you try to be.

Enjoying the Season

Fall is the most beautiful season, when the world comes alive with color. Don't let it pass you by as you rush about your usual routine. Besides admiring the colors, what are some of your favorite autumn activities?

◆ Sit outside with some blankets and a cup of tea to read a book, write in your journal . . . or just watch the leaves fall.

◆ Be thankful.

SCARLET MAPLE

Give Yourself a Day

Give yourself a natural day spa experience: Start the day with a long walk. Have a light breakfast of fruit and toast. Do yoga; go for a bike ride and/or more strenuous hike. Eat a good lunch followed by a luscious nap. Take an herbal salt bath in the afternoon. Get a massage and/or a manicure. Try Tai Chi Chuan, Qui Ghong, or meditation at the end of the day. Do it outdoors in your aromatherapy garden. Have a light dinner with only food from the garden. Go to bed early. The world can wait for just one day.

Checklist for Fall

It's fun to keep track of your area's weather and see how it impacts your garden. Although your climate may not be the same as mine, to get started, you can use my reminders of what to do when.

Typical Weather for Fall Months

	September	October	November
High/low temperatures:			
Rainfall:			
Any unusual weather patterns?			

September

Planting	Harvesting	Pruning	Doing	Preparing
❑ Put in a last planting of corn salad, lettuce, and radishes.	❑ Continue to harvest tomatoes and peppers.	❑ It's too soon to prune!	❑ Order fall bulbs and perennials from catalogs.	❑ Prepare foods for your freezer and pantry.
❑ Plant quick-growing cover crops such as crimson clover, hairy vetch, or buckwheat.	❑ Dig carrots and beets. ❑ Harvest winter squash.	❑	❑ Take notes on what did well in your garden. ❑ Make a dried flower wreath.	❑ Prepare your basement, toolshed, and storage areas to store your tools and furniture for the winter.
❑ Plant garlic cloves and multiplier onions.	❑ Enjoy the last fall raspberries.	❑	❑	❑ Make tomato sauce and salsa.
❑	❑ Cut dried sunflower seedheads or leave in the garden for the birds to enjoy.	❑		❑ Roast peppers.

October

Planting	Harvesting	Pruning	Doing	Preparing
❏ Plant fall trees, shrubs, perennials, and bulbs.	❏ Harvest the last chard, kale, broccoli, and cauliflower.	❏ Cut back perennials if you must, but don't cut back ornamental grasses until spring.	❏ Dig tender bulbs like cannas and store them if they don't overwinter outdoors in your area.	❏ Divide perennials.
❏	❏ Harvest grapes.	❏	❏ Take cuttings of geraniums and coleus for next season.	❏ Pile light mulch around tender perennials, herbs, and shrubs (lavender, roses, and so on).
❏	❏	❏	❏ Play in the leaves.	❏ Clean up the garden and start a new compost pile.
	❏		❏ Pot rosemary, thyme, chives, and parsley plants for your kitchen windowsill.	❏ Make applesauce.

November

Planting	Harvesting	Pruning	Doing	Preparing
❏ Move bushes and other plants in your garden once they go dormant.	❏ Check the garden for the last harvest of brussels sprouts and leeks.	❏ Use pine-bough prunings to decorate for the holidays. (When you're finished with them, spread them around your acid-loving plants.)	❏ Raid your freezer and pantry for Thanksgiving treats from the garden.	❏ Clean and set out bird feeders. Buy seeds and other bird-feeding supplies.
❏	❏ Pick American persimmons.		❏	❏ Mulch the strawberry bed with leaves or straw.
	❏	❏		❏ Prepare fig trees for overwintering in cold areas.
❏			❏	
	❏	❏		❏

New Year's Resolutions

It is always good to take time out to reflect and think about the past and what you want to do in the future. Set goals, make promises to yourself and others, and seek ways to get ever closer to the elusive goal of satisfaction and happiness.

New Year's Day is a great time to think about all this—after all, you're supposed to be making resolutions anyway. Make a few.

Think about It

I think you can spend your whole life looking or waiting for something else—and then you miss it because it was right in front of you the whole time. For some reason, gardening forces me into the present. It inspires me to make the most of what I have, enjoy it while it's happening, and anticipate the future as a pleasant surprise rather than an escape or some distant fantasy.

Resolve:

Resolve:

Resolve:

USDA Plant Hardiness Zone Map

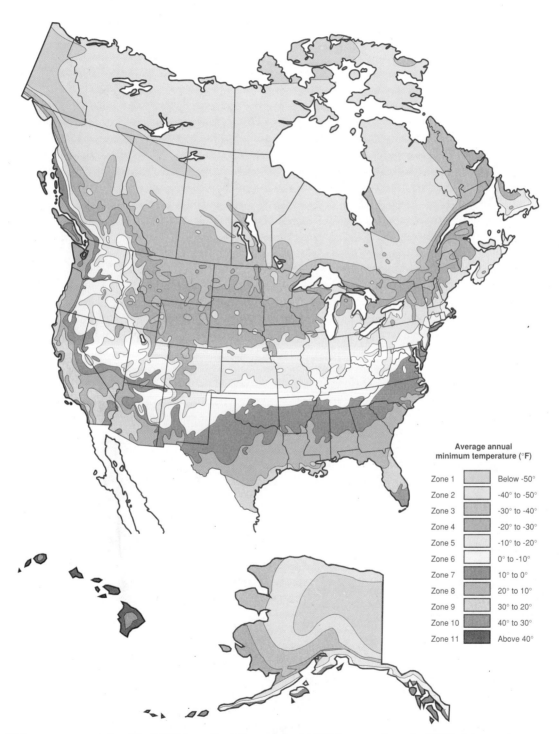

Average annual minimum temperature (°F)

Zone 1		Below -50°
Zone 2		-40° to -50°
Zone 3		-30° to -40°
Zone 4		-20° to -30°
Zone 5		-10° to -20°
Zone 6		0° to -10°
Zone 7		10° to 0°
Zone 8		20° to 10°
Zone 9		30° to 20°
Zone 10		40° to 30°
Zone 11		Above 40°

This map was revised in 1990 to reflect the original USDA map, done in 1965. It is now recognized as the best indicator of minimum temperatures available. Look at the map to find your area, then match its pattern to the key above. When you've found your color, the key will tell you what hardiness zone you live in. Remember that the map is a general guide; your particular conditions may vary.

SUNFLOWER